Ring
of
Dust

Ring
of
Dust

Louise Marois
translated by D. M. Bradford

Brick Books

Library and Archives Canada Cataloguing in Publication

Title: Ring of dust / by Louise Marois ; translated by D.M. Bradford.
Other titles: Trêve. English
Names: Marois, Louise, 1960- author. | Bradford, D. M., translator
Description: Translation of: Trêve.
Identifiers: Canadiana (print) 2025010699X | Canadiana (ebook) 20250106981 |
  ISBN 9781771316521 (softcover) | ISBN 9781771316538 (EPUB)
Subjects: LCGFT: Poetry.
Classification: LCC PS8626.A76 T7413 2025 | DDC C841/.6—dc23

Published by arrangement with éditions Triptyque, Montreal.
Originally published in French as Trêve in 2022.

We gratefully acknowledge the Canada Council for the Arts, the Government of Canada through the Canada Book Fund, the Ontario Arts Council, and the Government of Ontario for their support of our publishing program.

Canada Council   Conseil des arts   Funded by the
for the Arts   du Canada   Government
                                       of Canada

ONTARIO ARTS COUNCIL
CONSEIL DES ARTS DE L'ONTARIO
an Ontario government agency
un organisme du gouvernement de l'Ontario

Ontario

Edited by Oana Avasilichioaei.
Marois author photo by the author.
Bradford author photo by Annie France Noël.
The book is set in Utopia Std.
Design by Emma Allain.

Brick Books
487 King St. W.
Kingston, ON
K7L 2X7
www.brickbooks.ca

BRICK BOOKS

Though much of the work of Brick Books takes place on the ancestral lands of the Anishinaabeg, Haudenosaunee, Huron-Wendat, and Mississaugas of the Credit peoples, our editors, authors, and readers from many backgrounds are situated from coast to coast to coast in Canada on the traditional and unceded territories of over six hundred nations who have cared for Turtle Island from time immemorial. While living and working on these lands, we are committed to hearing and returning the rightful imaginative space to the poetries, songs, and stories that have been untold, under-told, wrongly told, and suppressed through colonization.

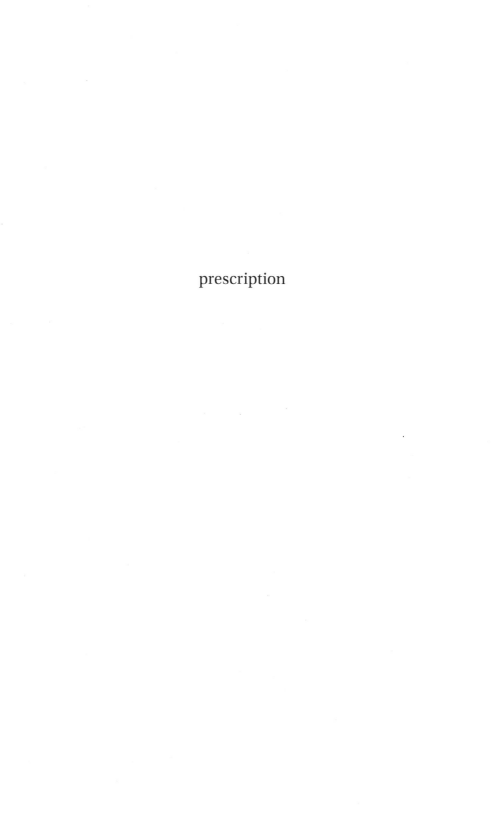

prescription

how does it feel to finally be loved
full of grief, no embrace[1]
on a night like this one
cresting a blood-red world

---

[1] *Aranea,* Latin for the spider biting my finger
the hurt is transfigured
flowers gone upside down

i'll talk about my mother
as if no one's listening at all
this damned tongue
foreign[2] to the both of us

i was telling you about yourself
about these words eating my heart out

---

[2] carpenter ants under my arm
i scoff beneath a brown and orange toque
square petals

dare to poke my head into your worries
into the thick bedspread its fragile[3] buds in relief
exhaustion

another propriety

---

[3] i trace a circle on the window with a marker
will know where the bird sets down
its habit of returning to the same spot

then to inaugurate[4] ourselves over and over again
i blow away
pistil after pistil
in each murmur a prowler
a guzzle of glands
a trickling coulis
the colour drains from my skin

---

[4] chair plants grow in a valley
Dominique Michel and Denise Filiatrault
put on a show
the black stripes' effect is a striking one

a duel among flies winds down under the lamp
its dancing glow speaks of hot, muggy days
of the impossible fusion
of flapping wings
brief escapes

attacks[5] and retreats
tiny victim
and the other one
alone
in the graveyard dawning

---

[5] miniature and pedunculate boxing gloves made of potato bits

rebuff
the plate into a thousand shards[6]
the gold lip sparkling as it falls
takes the harlequin pattern down with it
glaze and crumbs
the image of the couple in shrouds
unsettles the embossed crucifers a break
the cart, the carrot, and the fish
clumsily beheaded
what did you expect
this duel to reap

---

[6] i buy 249 army button-downs
find the neighbour's cat, his blistered scruff
i can't sleep, he snores

quiver at the new light
at the effluence of the low country
what remains memory aftertaste
would be there
stagnant
words only the workwoman[7] can dig up

---

[7] the yard is littered with binoculars and scissors
everything is rickety, weathered, my fear of staying stuck

got nothing if not a baking sheet[8]
in all its sovereign blankness
the lead firms in
a lack for the taking

on the edge of tears or a pond
alongside such sun
i expect to stop knowing at all

i lie down
where the stag hides out
on grass still flat from the weight of his gut
no more than you am i loved

---

[8] from the morgue i bring a wax-covered body home
blood-soaked paper
i offer After Eights to complete strangers

every moment of my life is a cozy bit of drama[9]

---

[9] my bike's broken derailleur
a western fair
in a bathing suit in the shit and grass
a mother and her disabled child
in the ear goes the banana

is that your visit[10] ruined
the sweet sound of the place as the sun begins to rise
the unhurried creatures who see you and smile
the light revealing the nuances of the light

is it the willow's crook that takes after your fall
the *ianthum* and *Rubus idaeus* gifted to the violets
and raspberry shrubs

is it being alone
before the you gets away from yourself

---

[10] i scour the sky find a bench and sit down
some kids wonder what i am, declare: she's a lesbian!

is it that[11]
what you leave unsaid
is to feed yourself memoir

---

[11] the Laurier pool, women swimming with their shoes on
i dive in to fish mine out

what good is so much solitude
in a sheer button-up, the effect
violently easy to grasp
scarring
of your halted sap
in my arms, empty fruit

the promise will never keep will have no
house nor nest
words up in the air[12]
envelop me in a muted sound
of confinement

---

[12] a woman cures my migraine under a pile of books
i buy a body of work for ten bucks
greasy, ancient manuscripts

am haunted by the animal child[13] carved into your grin
i run for it, scatter to the wind
when the rain smells of cow shit

---

[13] get bitten by a miniature stallion
explain to you it's actually a seahorse

she the instinguisher

long before now
way before me
your ruby lips a sublime arterial red

the fraudulent tongue perhaps

of this *nothing* you tell
only what it can[14] with gravity
forbidden
leaves me languishing

---

[14] metallic body glitter
your finger circles my belly button

nectariferous spur follicles
i want for every want, thirst
everybody for themselves mass grave earth

you were right
write it down
don't make our story up for myself

abstinence
i hush what could damage
what might come of the wreckage
oily palms

i return[15] my dirty hands
the writing
to the intimate destruction

---

[15] bohemian under a grey hide
i wander off

a pubic mound
supposedly where i come from
this bare
shadowy fold[16]
the knowing eye is a merciless one

---

[16] mysterious toys
my foot is a prothesis in the sand
i pull on black tassets, guitar and upright bass

the floral motif of the hours
everything, absolutely everything in a halo
majesty of the morning stroll
and still
to wander so far off it's impossible[17]

---

[17] kiss her to smell her breath
our marriage is annulled

the exact moment
to squeeze your hand crush it
cut the blood off[18]
and then some

that i be washed, cured of

---

[18] my eyelids scrub the back of my eyeballs
i beg my mother to recognize me

i imagine you ghostless
eye snug beneath the fur of lashes
the ravaged smell
plenitude in the flesh
atop a belly in its folds my head
busied[19]
to cry out by a thousand cuts

---

[19] we slip behind the window curtains

the pulse of your veins reassures me
you aren't far
you aren't
my nodular lungs
my tongue mid-swallow
horror returns
repels solitude
the inhospitable science[20] of breathing for two

---

[20] courted by huge sculptures of tourists
i don't understand anything

you laugh satirically irascibly
you laugh for another reason
knots in my hair
twists
the heavens tormented by our ugly bits[21]
i think
nothing warrants the taste of gummies

---

[21] on an invisible chair, up in the air
pussy in a net, out slips your tongue

i pop the burn open
not just poems but breasts
not just flesh for the predicates
the stories' skimming touch[22]

adjective for a leonine first name
winter flower

---

[22] high sea, amid coppery wreckage
i'm taken, dropped
deep in woods where two giant squirrels are hiding

to look[23] where there's no
to stay put where there's no

---

[23] i stub my cigarette on a woman's arm
she doesn't flinch
she says: flinching is just a habit

later,[24] in the oblique pastures
wings threading the warm air of summers
on a sloping bank the vertigo
exceedingly naked
i learn
to not waver
in the face of your screaming

---

[24] i'm encouraged to dive off a cliff
the clear water
paper lifebuoys

against your forehead
.deathly appropriate
the deflagration
woman coffin woman finitude
mere child of a child
no satin or essence of rare wood
smells of sulfur of wet dung
i have to[25] be born in the bad stuff

---

[25] i divert the trajectory of projectiles into my direction

i'm done waiting to come into this world
don't owe or feel
any pity[26] for the fallen fledgling
the throat-slit kitten in a fist
the poor bald sickly ox

---

[26] sharp curves
i move huge stones along the side of the road
fall into the ditch

prolix waters
i go deaf
shaky from crying
the air mangles the sightline
the light comes back all filthy[27]

---

[27] i visit the Plateau's hidden cemetery
sticks of incense for the chase

---

[28] a baroness opens her door to me, a crown of black locks

to repeat it to you without ever tiring of it
death enters[29] through the mouth

on the threshold of the waterline
a corpse gone soft

---

[29] a tractor bears down on me from behind
i push back with all my might

a day rises in turn
smashes its finger on the spectral appearance
of the branches, the oak and yew acorns
books keep me fed[30]

---

[30] a long way from the shore the calm water is a nasty brown
i scream: help!
i'm going to die, i just know it

mineral altar
russet leaves stewing in their juices
leather of maple, oats by the panicle
soaking in fluids
fruits of the sun
silt under my nails
and everything i'm thinking about
without writing it down

at the garden
salt ammonia soiled hay
i walk a calendar of dead leaves
the learned order[31] of plants in alignment
foretell collapse

i drag on[32]
in the unlikeness of the ground
its daughter

---

[31] i run through the forest
mama deer and her little ones make off
[32] to change my sex, my mother urges me

nothing that smells good forehead burning up
beauty would bounce back
am i still the object of
the inventiveness of your delights

tell me,[33] who hasn't whittled down
a weapon small enough to protect the child
in herself

---

[33] wads of chewing gum conceal our true personality

she the attractant

we work ourselves loose[34] bit by bit
a memory in a spiral
somewhere we're uprooted
lost for words
my lips feel you kiss them

---

[34] i move back in with my parents
take the fold-out bed
get some tiny pyjamas, a new stretchy material

the lukewarm blooming of the sky
the limits[35] of the bright miracle
i take a break from my tumbles, from words stumbled upon
i summon you with a touch of country verse
with what peels away the ugly
what would've been said all those wasted years
i'd so be up for it
would get drunk on the offering

---

[35] we consult psychiatrists, we're told to lower
our voices
we fold rags
a cork butt plug dangling from each

i confuse your absent voice
with the howling under the door
and all the necrosis that comes with it[36]
the lacks, ruins, unfulfillment, secrets
complete with a display
of pirouettes

---

[36] ejected from a submarine, i swim with other victims
a boy could make love to me were it not for this shirt between us

at the dep[37] on the deux 53
women talk
in front of the candy
talk about "diamond cut" g-strings
have you ever heard of such riches

---

[37] a baby out my ass is not a good sign
on the beach, Gaspesian-sounding couples go their separate ways

i study a drawing of a bare root
whereby the dirt soaks up the water
our lineage[38] all tangled up

---

[38] i read *Pour en finir avec Octobre*
the low ceiling of the cells, the nervous inmates, the riot
the nails that i pull up

you put, line up
your words in my bookcase mouth
how can confidence come
from that
from what it's made to swallow up

becomes perishable, rancid
my imagination

a fox trots past the Dairy Queen
i see big[39] when i write about you
lick my lips

---

[39] huge inflatable boat
thrill-seeking we buckle ourselves
into the craft
we're violently shaken, just a couple of kids

since the day began it's been on its own
no velvet throw to speak of
artifice
simply up and about
as you lay claim to being

got to
without which nothing is worth[40] writing down
streaks of hair burn out
the dog's voice gloopy from her stew

---

[40] to give birth
a litter of white balls of wool

the hollyhocks stare me down
styled[41] in an old-fashioned way, dusty rose
i, too, go shady and dried up

one step into the downy grass
the north licks the salt off my forehead
my face
gladly meets the calf's

---

[41] a man's head in my hands, i put it somewhere safe
leave it to rest

the greenery's words offer themselves up
i descend[42] into explaining leafing season to you
the achiness of goodbye muscles
cicada tinnitus
the glassine of eyelids
an oaf on parade i tell you all about
things i don't understand

---

[42] a doctor cures me standing on the table
after the operation, i write her, she lives at the psychiatric hospital

i expect everything from the landscape
spruce ivory
faded lilac
PVC chairs
it's a poem without you in it

the eternal target
the detonation
holes in the flesh of hours
to be honey or better
invisible to your horizons
to cut and run
in the joy that is the other

where[43] could i go without being there
without belonging to the place

---

[43] there's a party outside
i look for my underwear on the highway

to thrash about at dawn
our love-lost habits[44]
the radical certainty
that a stunted heart is bound
to never make it beyond us

---

[44] i'm the spinning top in the snow

we tell each other
and nothing but the truths[45]
are for telling
yours
all bloodthirsty, beheld from inside this

might there be such a thing
as a word necropolis

---

[45] rub down a huge stone with coal
i mimic the little black animals
cheek to cheek so breathtakingly beautiful

creatures with no beginning or end
no necessity or privation
you consider the forbidden words
what a waste[46] you would've said for anything else

the polished surface of our back-and-forths
doesn't begin anywhere
everything becomes precious except for us
i'd love to be the cultish thing

the wind claps its hands

---

[46] the Twinkie machine spits out
a ton of bills, suddenly i'm rich

rank

beneath a December rain
on the twentieth morning of the birth
a mother seeks to sever the cord
entangled in the white hair of her newborn
drained by so much viscosity and blood

inspects the fresh face she hopes to find pink and plump
then the mother's head falls back on the still-scorching pillow
—*o, hell no!*
and prays and Hail Marys for marble, plush drawing rooms,
naves, invented paradises and, above all, that this
moribund little creature
be balmed with graces posthaste
—*how gross you are*, declares the mother, *hideousness anew*

with all her boundless deference and despite her stupor
the mother broods the sticky grey egg
for herself and for her lord and saviour
the old midwife exhausted by the labour pains
torn all the way to the backbone
the nauseating wailing
struggles to shake off her tears and find the courage, the strength
for, at times, the mother aspires to subtract
this swampy female child from her sight
and valiantly untangles
the captive cord with her fingers
a ribbon of blood with which, nonetheless
she assembles such a clever knit
learned from her mother-grandmother
and all night she weaves her daughter's threads
the devoted, learned hands working to construct
and thusly heat the rooms of her soul
—*a tiny shelter of hemp and liquid scarlet*
to dress you in
will be all you get, you homely little thing
—*off with you, you sickening hatchling!*

local time whispers repulsion and she needles
the loops into each other as if a secular sacrifice
—*little to no pride for me, then, because of you, nor money*
nor merit not to mention the heavy cost to my bodily capacity
and prattles on to the child so the little one may memorize
what the mother is sacrificing for the nature she curses in her own way
—*you won't forget*
the mother puffs in the hollow of her crinkly baby ear
inflicting the fine squeak of penitence
—*you won't have anything neither,* she hisses again
her flushed face buried in her knit of the same red
a muscid with tartar-sheathed teeth
buzzes and weaves around them with grace and skill, a few small
helpings of skin, and cleverly pays no mind
to any of the mother's threats
as she desperately gives chase
with the juicy desire to squash it dead
—*if i catch you, i'll have you stuffed*
with your own ashes
and sends the fly sneaking under the blankets, rustling
the bleached cotton then hovering gayly above the newborn
and stinging her violently once more
—*leave her be why don't cha, leave her alone!*
screams the woman, swinging her knitting needles
—*curse me instead, you ghoul, me, lowing forebear stock*
come taste this unfortunate, empty flesh, come on
you shit fly, she continues
stable fly
bean fly
spotted fly
robber fly
olive fruit fly
blue bottle fly
carrot fly
blow fly
you shit fly, shit fly, shit fly of shits!
and with what little strength she has left
she weeps again, quietly, between what loops

she manages as milk hisses in her breast
the room closing in, the walls huddling up against them
and in this new misery that heralds little gaiety
little rest, she dries the youngling
sets her on the bedroom windowsill
and gripes
—*you mustn't wither like your older brother,*
my unspoken sorrow would be so complete, so plain to see
but the mother cannot contain her tears, a slow net
of melancholy cast
atop the child's tummy

out her bedroom window, the mother sees a path
laid out before them
no trees no thicket, simply the dullness of reality
—*December babies have no destiny*
she puffs, a voice soggy and soft
so well does she engulf the child in her worries
that the body rises like a good leaven loaf
the child appears for her future baptism, first day
of year sixty-one, golden and just about round enough
the mother admits
skin so starchy it furrows the waxy brow of the cleric
this old billy goat who dares, with fingertip
and tongue cracked by a gluttonous taste for the host offering,
to draw a splash of holy water from his marble clamshell
for the child's soft forehead
—*and what shall be her name?*
he asks the mother with the impatience of a solitary man
but thankfully for both her and the newborn
the freshly repainted chapel ceiling conceals the fetid breath
of the likely sexless priest
—*once baptized, this little rug rat will lord over just as well*
as any ass-to-trumpet cherub dangling
above your head
answers the mother, with a snotty look
—*Rank, her name is, will be, Rank*
and he, as any goodly ignorant priest, daubs her with hits of the censer

and aspergillum, grumbling that there is no rhyme or reason to it
the child, who'd barely made a peep if any, instead feeling
a dribble on her forehead and in her name the goodness
of a delicious marzipan offering glazed in royal icing
which the mother prepared for the babe
—*despite it all, a good mother you make*
rules the cleric jealous of her womanly authority

as soon as the priest retreats into his sacristy, the shimmer
of a cross upon his back in all its embroidered majesty
the mother sticks the child's few ounces of flesh under her arm
tucks them deep in her pea coat between blankets and keys
no muscid this time
and heads back down the centre aisle, something
of a metronome's precision
about her gait

back home, in lead chalk, the mother draws a portrait
of her third little bean on the back of a calendar
intent on the task and determined to copy certain details
of the one who was to wear the emblem of the next decades
the shiny metallic linework that confers
upon the young face
nothing of a panacea, but still makes, all told, for a handsome spirit
Rank, despite wearing the habit of her young age, suddenly grasps that it
is her in fact
and has not the slightest doubt of her wretchedness[47]

---

[47] crusty toilets yet again, i flee the premises
a silver medal between my butt cheeks

my selfishness is pure

without a word
i speak to the unknown she
to the shapeless regalia[48] of an inhospitable belly

---

[48] i encourage them to get top surgery
sights set on a desert island, i wear pink lipstick

i linger
over the gnarled perfume of your scarf
worn-out
and suddenly[49] subterranean
a lodge welcomes me in

the leaves drip
noon at work in the fields
the fleeting September soil
the open arms of balance
cardinal veins before me

---

[49] the wood floor ripples its way out
of the store
forces us to leave

---

[50] the growers change their minds, they won't be
farming our land
too noisy
for once that there was something to celebrate

first the window, which the ear can't see
then we drank
we took apart[51] our story

---

[51] we cook up lilies out of frost, gift them to each other

i talk to myself about solitude
about your nudity
so what[52] if none of it can bear or seed
entanglement

who am i once night
closes in

---

[52] i make my home on clay
a kid at the lookout snuggles up to me

red, dominant, indisputable
the swelling skirts[53] of the pads
the hygiene of tongues

in the mouth of coats of arms
everything you say about it
is just that
the hopefulness of a tongue

a swallow's girl
i feed on insect voices
on cocoon repair
might this be the creation of the end

sudden confines of forgetting
i make do without a place a date a baptistry
the gold of gaudy charms
what exactly
is a sparkling smile

---

[53] a tsunami
dinosaurs come from all over
we make love, swaddled in bubble wrap

and then, your reluctances
i'd like the house round
i'd like it all original[54] and a glade
to ripen the dew's influence
the heat that settles between two doors
the crunch of pebbles

---

[54] leaves sprout up all along my fingers
i prune them, look after them
flee the student girl

instead of these stories
captive
throat in the belly
you listen to the falling rain

i'll write you down[55] to make the clouds speak

---

[55] i lose track of my things
every doorknob pulls off in my hand

a bit lower down rusty snares
hanging from the hemlock, traps
we'd stuff[56]
the eyes, blood rubies
a couple of marbles to hush all veracity

---

[56] a hook in the throat ensures the quality of my death
like a fish on *The Nature of Things*
hanging in a closet

in the hollow[57] of ancient words i exhaust myself
indiscriminately
which reveals my deliverance

have no lookout or guiding star
might we not make a party out of lightning bugs
in a bouquet above my poor papers
the tarnished flower won't ever be a rag

---

[57] i hesitate to jump off the bridge
mould floats to the surface

to tallow[58] the oblique openings
your presence would bring a warm touch
cinnamon wine and downy feet
in the middle of Midnight Square
i implore the hours
make it all new again

---

[58] covered in potato bugs
a steak knife to remove them

mother of my body

who will cheer me up as much as dumb me down
or else[59] my woolen joy
on a white and bitter day
on a single day forgotten
down to the bone

---

[59] photograph of a white flower at the foot of an exotic tree
morning sky a shadowy hue

the stupefying sun tendrils its triumphant rays
furrows the earth with our one shot at existence
we disappear,[60] prudish with allusions
the dead girl's garden, vacant

the shadow is at our bedside
the hours snug with worrying

---

[60] i, too, wear a long robe, a cornette on my head
a beach leads way out to a reef at sea

i will it
go looking in a moment of stillness, the only logic pendulates
to write is poison
same as a hollowed-out tree,[61] but still standing

---

[61] no doors, but tubes for stairs, traps for hares
the air kicks the sand up and scours it
we watch from the window, useless

the blue staircase cascades me down
high chamber of grief[62]
place for all the departed
the only child i have
that i didn't
have
yours

---

[62] a polar bear and her babies penned in the apartment
one idea for bothering the landlord

no room
in your irreparable rapture
i get out of bed
for the dream of getting out of it
the blossomed blood of the dogwood
i get up in time for hugs and kisses
that short-lived transparency
is this my truth or the illusion of it
we gather pages, fire, into mountains
clever about nothing at all

October burns
the illness of time never far off
hazy, i sneak a look
ambition[63] is a trap
to be moved would be
to succumb

---

[63] 5 p.m. at the Florida airport
the locked door is a huge glass overcoat

what gives me shelter, gives me family
my young-breasted wet nurse[64]
sweet larva
no sleep under the old rags
who will carve me a lullaby
lips like a glistening worm

---

[64] in a shipping container, i soar above the sea
it's sunny out, i land softly
the cookie jars each the shape of a mouth

place unmoored from matter
our house[65] sprouted up
between the weeds and chunks of gravel
the beige of futile things and blesséd liquor
i judged
you, September

---

[65] an empty room, i swing from nylon straps
tied around my elbows

where am i in this forest with nothing vernal about it now
the night calves[66]
its icy stars
so close
i forget everything else

---

[66] a fly with a large oral cavity
eats with its nutcracker pincers

it's not so much the malice in words
as their ominous nature
souls on the scale

the sumptuousness of being nothing[67] but hands
the landscaped plenitude of gardens without geometry
floral displays, simply
neither blood nor abundance
thick milk of imaginary flowers

---

[67] i caress a tiny head just above the ground, no body
winter of dead children, trail of the stain

resplendent time
between sleeping and awake
deserted
done believing in the excess of laughter[68] and tears

lights fade into the trees
i long for the coming shadows, the thread of patience
snow will come, the sky is so cold now

---

[68] a drawing suffered a heart attack, bad moment
to write a short story, title: "Kills Alone"

nesting words, shacked up
where tongues slumber

tell me, can you hear them mingling with your guts
enough cells for love and hate
i have words in my feet my eyes
stuff of silk stone of alder of the first frost
please help me

tell me, can you hear them up in my keep
their shade more tinctorial than it's ever been
we can't help[69] but kill them

---

[69] the shadow in perfect harmony with the angle of the sun
i rip it to pieces

tongue coated
poorly digested
ancient worm-eating woman
even half-starved i'd find something to spit[70]
and i feast beneath the rubric
high poetess of the penniless

---

[70] our neighbours torturers burglars dance with me
the bedroom is nicer in mustard
returned from so far afield they forget what language we speak

slipping in my own blood
where are the drownings of my dreams
my culminations[71]

never a beginning

---

[71] physics between medicine and precinct
individual Kraft Singles on which to write
i won't do it

the arrival of melodies Sundays up my faith
reversible, deforested
to set you in stone and rub up on you, to polish us
now nothing stands its ground
you, my one and only reason to reach[72]
the misty foothills of the firmament

---

[72] no one doubts that i'm a woman
at the summit, everything is sad

we live in the midst of sunless burrows
nests threaded way up in the trees
families of insects all around us
we live on the same well-worn trail as the deer
as the bright linework of the spider
we live on partridge crap, on the turds
of cats
voles and caterpillars
on the jay's discarded eggshells
we live with the fly circling us at the counter
with the worker ant everywhere
we sleep with the blackbird's song, the chipmunk's calls
we strut about sans panache or plumage
claws or hooves, antennae or wings
i imagine them on my back, off my forehead, around my ankles
and without knowing it
i kill everything i step on

splendour in the distance
ear-splitting words that return
me to grief
i hear voices, and they help me
ease my dependence[73]
the distance reaches me, sears me white hot
a palate petted
a low flame's purifying touch

---

[73] to want to live in the basement
a bag of potatoes every month

everything trips me up
with these bones of coal and chalk
the tiniest step on the page is glorious
hobbles the hazard[74]

---

[74] inseparable fem sweethearts slung on my back
i keep shovelling

vein gone blue from the weight of the axe
i hack through photo books
will defend them a hundred times over
i talk to myself[75] between the cords
like i write myself
lines of verse for the stove

---

[75] a young woman says she's tired
i put her in a crib under a countertop

the trees yammer on
soft babble[76] of leaves and needles
hymn i regret as the murmurs of trees drop
so much commotion beyond here
so much so
there's no place left to hear nothing at all

---

[76] a little girl on my hip
the carafe slides off the level tabletop

the house shuts its eyes again
its labyrinth
where its sun washes my shadow's child[77]
now nothing comes before me
i'm unfulfilled

i scare myself, lungs dirty with screams
pit of black thread
dragging on in these wounds
i carry my uncertain delight

---

[77] my leg skin is too big
try clothespins, they tell me

i ran aground against the flank of a tree
the guts of a rock
i shattered the purple wind, an ox song[78]
the smoky halo of a tin roof
i scorched my eyes on beauty
i split the blood of a maple down to its useless cabinetry
today i pray tomorrow
hung up on the same gnarled horizon
hope leaks and I'm stuck in it
eve of a joy that won't be that hasn't ever been
no window
no door keeps out the night
it enters, blood red
by way of the contours of my cool head
saps the ink of the passages
twilight shrouds me in its layers

---

[78] at the opera
sometimes a bad impression
rotten eggs, the hen is ill

unction

the forest[79] beginning of an end
has me so scared that i doubt myself
i have neither the courage nor ambition for enclaves
i hold on to the dreams of my green nights
like the fear that i'll needlessly wake up
between layers of light

---

[79] $300 for a hacienda-pantry-style bookcase
moved, i christen it the scarlet owl

words slip in and out
whittled sublimated
visit and unearth me
i become frequentable

to write to the tune of raucous
loudmouth words, the ones that revive me
sources of affliction and worry
to face off with[80] the brimming ink

everything is perfectly chewed up
my cuticles
my lips

---

[80] rub up against me to catch it, she says, an allergy

canoness of the dawn
workwoman of the seed rosary
frost of the moon
back of the blade
would build a meal

empty belly[81]
furtive
silent around the eyes
beak ready for your pecks
i have neither the words nor the breasts

---

[81] two poodles following a passerby
folds up her bra to carry them

it's not the injury that hurts
it's not knowing who it makes me
and i'm pleine[82] of these injuries
in my timbered heart, not one of them
is spared
from the instant repulsion
they require of me

---

[82] my memory isn't bilingual!

infrangible and iniquitous
the shadow concedes that she means to not be me
merchant of storms
that as day and night fritter away
everything i write about you erases me
eats away[83] at me
with unbelievable glee

the fist's resolve
versus these funereal ornaments
i forget how to weep for myself
so i weep for you

---

[83] miniature metal coffin under my narrow bed
white sheets
and too small a pillow

to eat drink alone is an invalidating act
displeasure
of the passed-out[84]
whereas yesterday everything was intoxicating
i leave dirty plates all over the place
as if the fête really did fête
the smell of blown-out candles is meat off the grill

---

[84] wood hallways protect the sky's blue base
pebbles in flowery bedsheets

my loneliness born of another
partisan place
comes from nowhere else but you
everything outside of that is nonsense

who makes up the stuff of silence[85]
what's the nature of its primary vocation
you put it on
shake out every limb
in yesterday's green moss
your nails black with freedom

---

[85] i take flight without ever hurting its ears

the ground erased from the drawing
i hope for a trace
me, shadowy and petrified
another step and i shoot
dead, not dead[86]

---

removed from myself[87]
in the patient hours
i stay put

i give you my word
you won't hear a thing
i'm babbling
everything is pointless
and more than ever
poetry

---

[87] women with shaved heads, sequins
dance on a platform
invite a skeletal dog to drink

who exactly has a normal shape
i must've lost mine, never had one
the nightmare rushes[88] into the night
the words into impertinence
the radio talks, sings
rots my brain

---

[88] i sleep on a King Chopper scale model
with a long, padded seat
an eagle perched on the backrest

show how it's done[89]
in metaphors or actions
a simple
unassailable indication
of my mothball and nettle temperance
who's with me

---

[89] they examine my shoulder with a magnifying glass
a childhood accident

frugally
i'll put the matter to the grindstone
as i might[90] the curd of
a too-crazy, too-forbidden desire

---

[90] pubic mound freshly shaved
looks like a cucumber seed

girl once removed by birth
daringly
i elude the problem of entertaining myself
every catastrophe is an interruption
unimagined matter[91] of words
the art of thinking would be to write

---

[91] a chunk of my tooth, i fix it
everything is awesome

a chip off the old moon
in the twelfth month of the year
timeline of mysteries
have i been lured away from my senses
an old-timey joke
o tragedy[92]

---

[92] among elderly ladies
one of them spews all her hate at me
hear her out with the sole desire to get away

the moment softens years of nasty anniversaries
everything can be defused, as far you see it
my gaiety like a syllable descends[93]
only citalopram can knock me out

---

[93] a papier-mâché hat, Queen Elizabeth's

my fragile, illustrious insurrections
i go toe to toe with the wind
with the legends to tend
the peony maws to straighten out

born of a molehill
isolated hillock
shaped by nature's hand[94]
the only heights i picture for myself

---

[94] i sniff a teddy bear, then stretch it out
a nipple

mad eye

the true grandeur of the seasons
a garden in a circle of stones
the sun's bare hands
a woman fallen in the slow tracks of cattle
trails torn up by torrents
with not the slightest rescue in sight
the storm makes itself heard
a short while, in its awful violence
crashes down liquefies
the woman, without the means to be more
than witness to her own misfortune
fingers in her mouth, crying
the woman, amid her wailing
—*i'm learning to die learning to die*

racket of waters
throttled foliage, screams
roars reach the heavens
mercilessness mutilates and panics
upturned earth in the filthy diffuse light
grey rollers drawn over the horizon
a respite
then again and again and again
the howling wind of her prayers
in the distance death and a little girl
try to save her cat from drowning
under the nails, slipstream, moraine
the girl lying flat, at the end of the dock, frantic
her feet her arms thrashing
a rescue fit for a person
she gets a hold of the beloved, frightened feline
on the edge of death
which could come for him at any moment

in his box, floating and sopping, drifting
spuming waves
sweep away
the child's light body

her clenched fist and flesh
battered by the impetuous current

after the storm the sky
fills with loathsome old blue-pinks
clothes shimmer
on bodies

a farmer searches for his wife
the stirred air fogs over
eye of bad weather
curses, hounds everything, her as well as he
worries
she, neither in the cowshed
nor at the garden well
he gets agitated and screams out with three maws
mad nature against him
and screams and screams
great big trees have lost limbs
bark torn off
vast whirlwinds swarming with dark birds
the moment has flesh in knots
the old man empties himself out
his apprehension his feet alert
from one building to the next
helps his hefty animals along
counts, attentive, pats haunches
cries out his wife's name
his animals', his wife's again
many times over, steps without knowing it
near and atop her, his wife, her head
his bovine heart
his wife, her head, her heart, shatters
without knowing it, her bones
her long straw-coloured hair
her lovely long back
one boot and hoof at a time
stamps shit down squashes her sinks her in

when finally, his youngest
a soiled scrap of fabric between her fingertips
white flowers between grey and silt
lets him have it
the old man cries
like a newborn
near her atop her, the newborn man
collapses
to better curse, condemn himself
he whom trouble follows
smack dab in the middle of disunity and chaos
scorns, despises himself
she, his love, fairy from the first
now taken by alluvia
without ever relenting
promises, grants himself a dead man's face
no more pity
feels nothing, the coward
is worth nothing
no more comings into the world
and faces what he is

packs a basket with explosives the departed's ashes
a ladder against the tin shingles
his girl on his back
pushes her up
says
—*late wife with the ear the eye sediment*
blaring day of fiery artifice
funereal mortar shell, give my regards to the irreparable firmament

the little one distraught for two
heel-kicks the shingles
tries to rid herself of her brimming exaltation
perched on the barn roof
the war between the two
worsens
he lights the fuse

time for deflagrations
a dazzling ring of dust
blankets bottomless prayers
stink of sulfur and wet dung in the air

he says
—*grave-woman, my one and only*
gnaws his scrap of fabric
picks his teeth with it
the girl, her pallid face, just like his
horror pierces her skin
the father hears nothing
scrapes himself rusted to the bone

life labours on, unchanged
the father drifts away from her as from himself
puts his aversion to the test, forces himself
to put on his wife's dirty white dress
dappled with her flowers
wears the thing, this minder's frock
in the fields at the well to the barn
he wears it down mends it with devotion
white brown tinder fungus
longs for her flourishes to blossom upon him
each squealing beneath his touch, in ruins
patient, he'd wait for them

each dawn, he raises his arms puts the dress on
obeys himself
the girl helps him
all too gently
hushes nourishes the shakes and tears, she knows
she teases his bulging neck vein
with long and sluggish pecks
she, so slight, watches him

he wants to vanish from her sight
but can't

the girl, for her part, knows how to run sleep in the pasture
arm-wings gliding on the warm air of the moment, she knows
without wavering, standing tall, on a vertiginous slope
knows not to fall
knows the imagined flight of untameable bodies
through and through
knows to run beneath the weight of nightly murmurs
she says to him
—*my little gaudy-hearted flower*
you're terribly cute in your hideousness

rests her hand on him a bouquet
she keeps an eye out, he holds his breath
stops living one instant and then another
without shyness or modesty
she considers his timeworn silhouette
cheeks plump with promises
looms steadily closer
to the undignified and revolting
sniffs bedspread heavy paws at the fragile buds
now boiling hot
—*are you burning up?* she asks
capable of hatred, of bone-tiredness
she doesn't dare remember his worries
guarded, she frightens and dominates
so very gently toward this, the mess
she says
—*goddamn it, damn you and cry for your own damn sake*
she spits at him
—*i'm telling you, give it a good cry*
without ever escaping the bodies they are
—*you're gonna cry for yourself, right?*
the two of them in the cracks and smears of the heart
in the belly's debris
the father comes undone, pistil after pistil
inaugurates himself over and over again with each of his swells
her anger and their wounds
and she prowls

murmurs endless forevers to him
she tells him
—sweetness, the hairy trouble that started in your throat
gone as deep as your glands
she rubs his gums teeth with her index finger
and lower down where skin sheds its colour
annihilation numbs all over
lowers his soiled underwear
over his thighs, over every bead of skin
beneath eyes nodules the forbidden
she hates him spectacularly
holds onto the horror
and returns, repelled by his rattling
his death rattle again
breathing for two
lungs filthy with closeness

in her room, the fear of dreams
vaulted, she eyes night falling
alone with the cross on her chest
sitting on her bed
in inhospitable silence
delicately opens the padded lid
lake-wood jewelry box
presses her lips, her cheek against the greeting cards
loves violently
which she fears
which shines in the hollow of her palms
this routine burn
rough dust of pasted colours
that remind of her father's cheeks
tiny specks of light right in the mad eye[95]

---

[95] she's dead, but won't die

no title[96]

---

[96] the woman so tall so slim
she crouches down on her sole foot

litter of words
how to be born another way than that

meagre December in the mist
no snow no cold no feathery crystals
a bed i can neither lie in nor get out of

incandescent stillness
to unfurl you with a secret[97]
i'll speak to you with abandon
my goddess alone
knows how to calm me down

---

[97] too long in a belly
the head deformed, my aneurysmal sex

the verses tire themselves out
mean and miserly
i hoard every coin i can
lift myself out of the ordeal
wrench free with my every leap
the floral idea is astringent to me
elliptical[98]
in vain, i cover you up

---

[98] an hour walking up a rope ladder

obscurity walls me off
imposes the seduction of dreams
upon waking, everything tears me down
from the truest to the most wrong
its indeterminate language is strange to me
well-versed in the immaterial[99]

the day is unassailable
is my confinement
my shortcut to why i'm here

---

[99] the mercury melts in my grey-skinned palm

words are prepared, embalmed
warmed up, lined up nose to tail
i connect vocable particles
promises of promiscuity[100]
spread and spread
unbreathable, turned blood red

---

[100] i scream: Mom! she appears in her nightgown

i pass out
ordinarily
in isolation
my constructed solitude

have my father's hands[101]
their old-man strength
hands incapable of forgiveness
i have my father's hands of another time
never my mother's
despising forgiveness

---

[101] shred the paper of his face, my fingers through his eyes
spruce felled in summertime

deep throat, snug neck
self-worth
to get lost[102] for a new road

the flowers's sap
the bees's haul
the fruit's ink
and me
in the kindled flame failure's augury[103]

feathery beasts stir and flap
know, for their part, what's for the best

---

[102] lake, on a raft headed out to a reef just below the surface
i paddle with an eyeglasses case

[103] holding my breath i catch an exotic bird
green, gold, and black, its mother pecks my finger
kids-only restaurant

i turn[104] on myself
i'm a reef at your window
worried about the shattered wind
about time whispered in the open
about the belatedness of the dying

---

[104] if i sit at the back of the canoe, we sink
a lifeless partridge at the bottom of the lake
worms slither over its feathers

the delirium of deliverance
gives way to fever
but who[105] will long for this time
as it runs out on us

---

[105] a bouquet of a single kind of flower
a woman on the side, in a blue chenille dress

outside
like a sun refusing its place
the pallor of skirted lampshades
my regret[106] is that i can't see higher
than inside myself at night

---

[106] we throw out still-wrapped gifts,
the accountant is beside herself

flowers buried in the front yard
snowy with sleep you speak coldly
of this beauty no longer
your breath[107] touched
by its indivisible white fruit

i don't see don't partake
according to my position or opposition
i receive the faintest glimmer that makes me see
from whom it conceals me
akin and transparent

---

[107] a cat plays with its head, nerves dangling
hair done and made up i pose, what for, i have no idea

i write into the void
the sun[108] melts
don't have the time have no time at all
i only have this coat of a landscape

rain deprived of this day
because i don't write
when obsession
deprives me of my devotion

---

[108] hundreds of red fans all over the ceiling

my little study, conversations
adjacent to my stockpile[109] of painful keepsakes
from my continent dreams
i knead the blood of things

a single word captured
mid-flight
it feeds me[110]
my notebook's stomach so full
i can barely keep going

---

[109] my skin rolls beneath my fingers
the caisse populaire keeps my money deep in the lake

[110] crushed eggshell salad

i repaint the heavens, its ghosts
dreams slip out of the tapestries
my realities aren't mine to choose

the delight that interrupts me[111]
same as my animal appetite and wine
no longer suffice

---

[111] i get into an argument with a fish, i swim under the ice

i clear my throat, the grass
of my sixtieth year
the round eye of the melancholy cow[112]
the sown earth tossed under the Christmas tree

oily phloem of the first sculpted hours
your face
in a few moments
i take every angle for a sweet risk

---

[112] black line under each eye
i need to go home, my shoes in a trailer somewhere

i regret the words night, incense, round
the ones i belonged to

lord
to come out of the womb[113] talking about a flower
an empirical and peaceful message

---

[113] little wall of snow, brothel for women, the climax of a stranger

scraps

114

---
[114] my parents watch each other die
bitterly reject each other's suffering

---

[115] a garter snake stuck in a crack in the floor

---

[116] my meds on the back seat
a doctor on a trampoline

117

---

[117] a witch dances, her stomach flat against a wall

---

[118] i run on the ice, tiptoe my feet

[119] handbags made out of German army helmets
marble headstone armoire

[120] i demand the real definition of the word "parmesan"

,

---

[121] in winter, i help a lady, slide my fingers into a slit
she finds me ugly without eyebrows

---

[122] i look for a plastic cow in a toy store

---

[123] oakum rope over my shoulder

---

[124] a young man is carrying a blond rabbit, half-inflated

125

---

[125] the farmer wriggles, a marionette now nothing more than a wooden stick

164

---

126 a hand under the door helps me yank up some old linoleum
i pull a piece up, another appears

[127] hundreds of beds lined up, hundreds of multicolour bedspreads

---

[128] a man walks a giant rainbow-coloured bird on a leash
the insides pulled out, save for the heart
throws himself into a Longueuil-bound canal with his son

---

[129] my mother will die in a week
i carry her across rue Saint-Denis

130 got a job in an ad agency where everything is ugly

[131] three women in their thirties, well-armed, want me dead
i have a gun, one that melts hair, hot syrup

---

[132] i don't consent to the medical procedure
to get the baby out only to return it into the uterus
and birth it again

---

[133] i inherit a country house, someone's there
there's light under the door, the washing machine is on
the man moves out, takes the sink with him, leaving a gaping hole
his face is a wad of chewing gum

[134] for the journey i roast a chicken in my backpack

---

[135] with little, blue-black fruit, i make necklaces
once they've been cooked

---

[136] every morning a woman makes a $1,500 deposit, we try to figure out who

---

[137] i remove the legs of every piece of furniture
my gun is just a branch covered in Saran Wrap

the end[138]

---

[138] we light up monuments
the actual opacity
there where withered stars burn out
without rotting

Contents

Acknowledgments

To Nicholas Dawson, for bringing this to me. And to Triptyque, for making it an easy, happy turn.

To Alayna Munce, always, for being more than open to this, for inching us forward and forward and forward.

To Louise Marois, for the words, foremost—for the myth-making, the slanted, opaque layers, and for talking it out generously, always answering my curious questions, later.

To Oana Avasilichioaei, my editor, for pouring over all of this work with me after the fact.

The publication of any translation, let alone a translation of poetry, is a massive reminder of the unlikely care and patience and faith that goes into all this. I wanted to translate *Trêve* because I had hardly ever found anything lusher, more circuitous, more literal and physical in its opaque layers. Which is to say, the decision to take this work on was purely personal, emotional, writerly—the desire to work out the paces of Marois's eerie stripping out of gender, of love, of relationships good and bad, of the many selves. And Nicho at Triptyque, Alayna at Brick Books, Louise and Oana between the pages with me—they just went for it, believed I'd carry it through.

There are no books like this without a certain sweet weakness for this kind of leap. I hope that means something to you, too.

D.M. Bradford

Louise Marois is an acclaimed writer and artist born in Montreal in 1960. Recognized for her poetic works many times over, her first collection of poetry received the Jacqueline-Déry-Mochon prize and she has twice been a finalist for the Governor General Literary Award. She lives and works in Sherbrooke, Quebec, where she dedicates her time to writing and artmaking.

Darby Minott Bradford is a poet and translator. They are the author of the hybrid poetry collection *Dream of No One but Myself* (Brick Books, 2021), which won the A.M. Klein QWF Prize for Poetry, and was a finalist for, among others, the Griffin Poetry Prize and Governor General Literary Awards. Bradford's first translation, *House Within a House* by Nicholas Dawson (Brick Books, 2023), received the VMI Betsy Warland Between Genres Award and John Glassco Translation Prize, and was shortlisted for the Governor General Literary Award for Translation. Their most recent book of poetry, *Bottom Rail on Top*, was a Raymond Souster Award finalist. Bradford lives and works in Tio'tia:ke (Montreal) on the unceded territory of the Kanien'kehá:ka Nation.

Printed by Imprimerie Gauvin
Gatineau, Québec